I0463905

ASSHOLE SERIES

Amusing Swear Words To Color

For Stress Releasing

By

Queenie McJody

Happy Coloring!

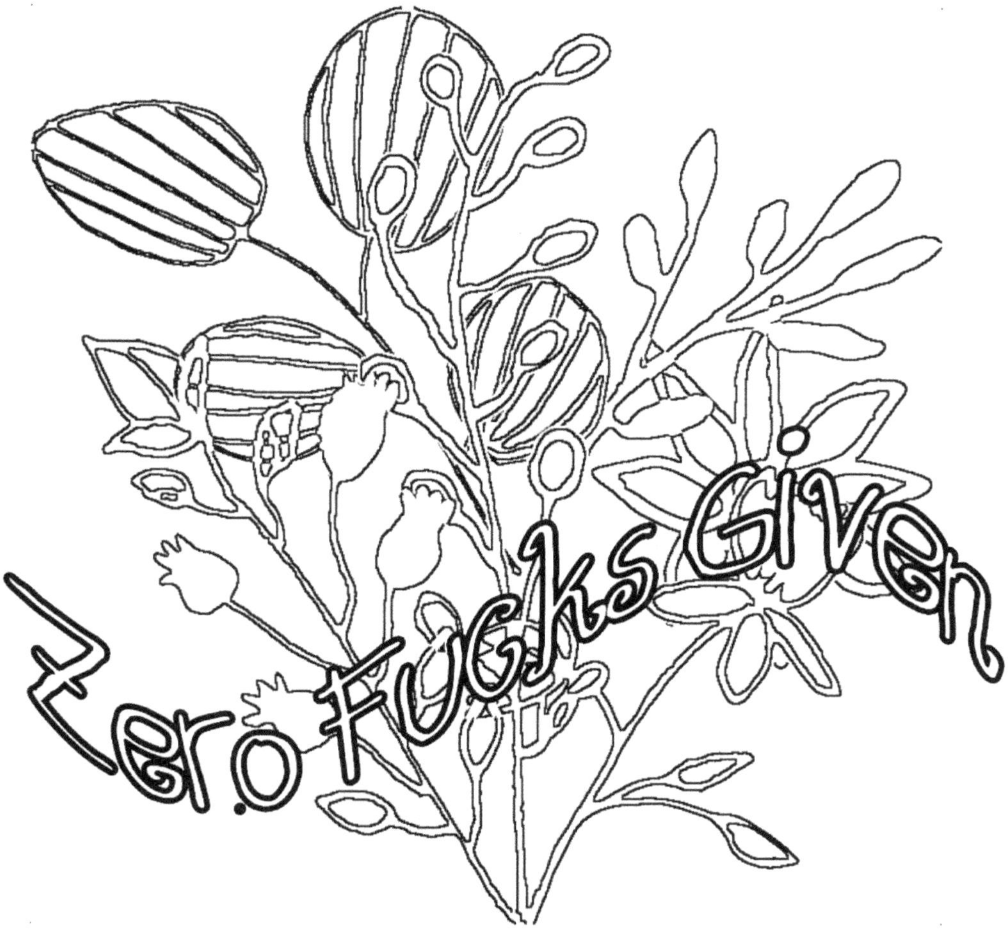
Zero Fucks Given

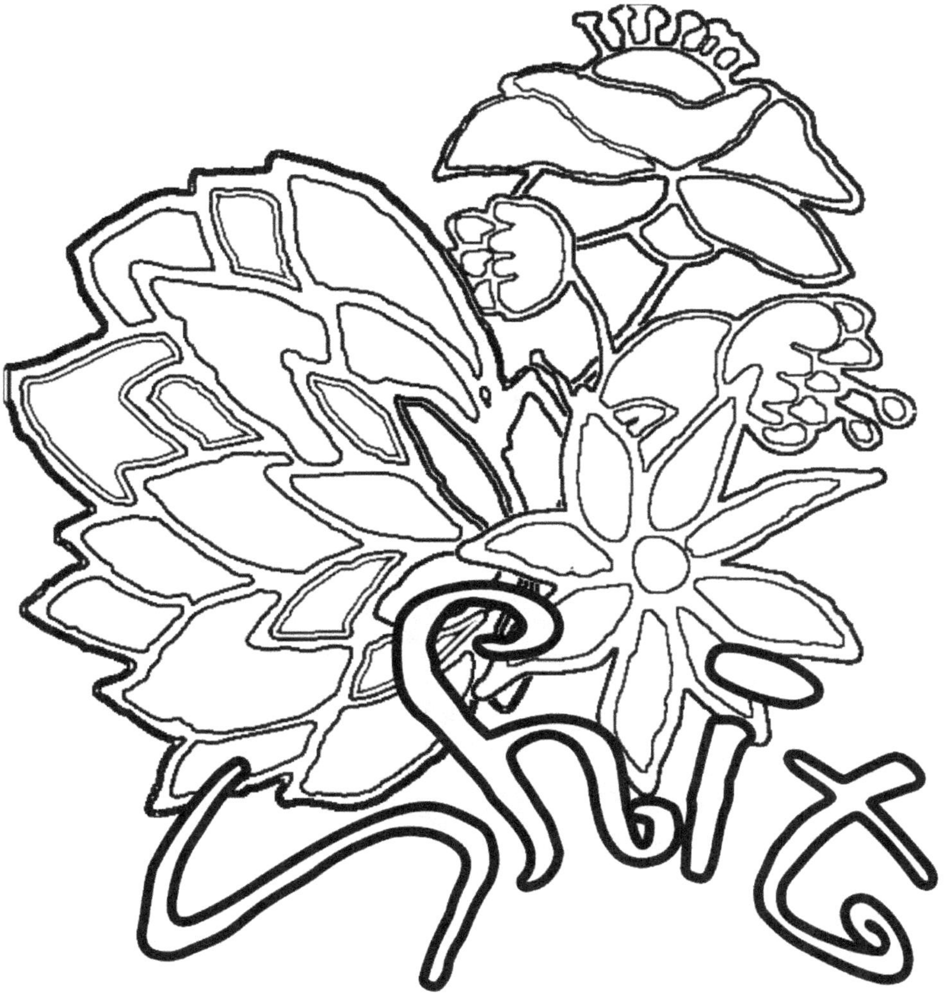
Shit

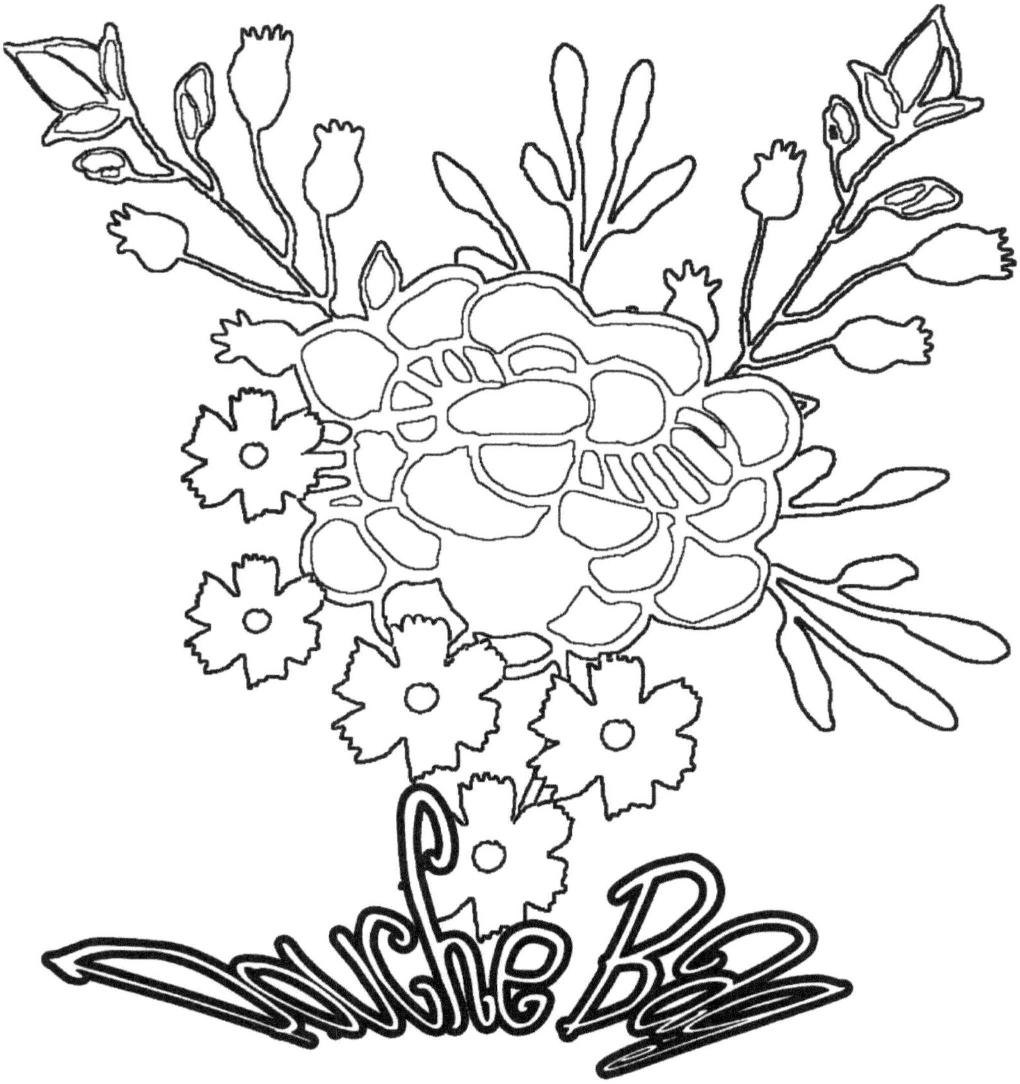
Douche Bag

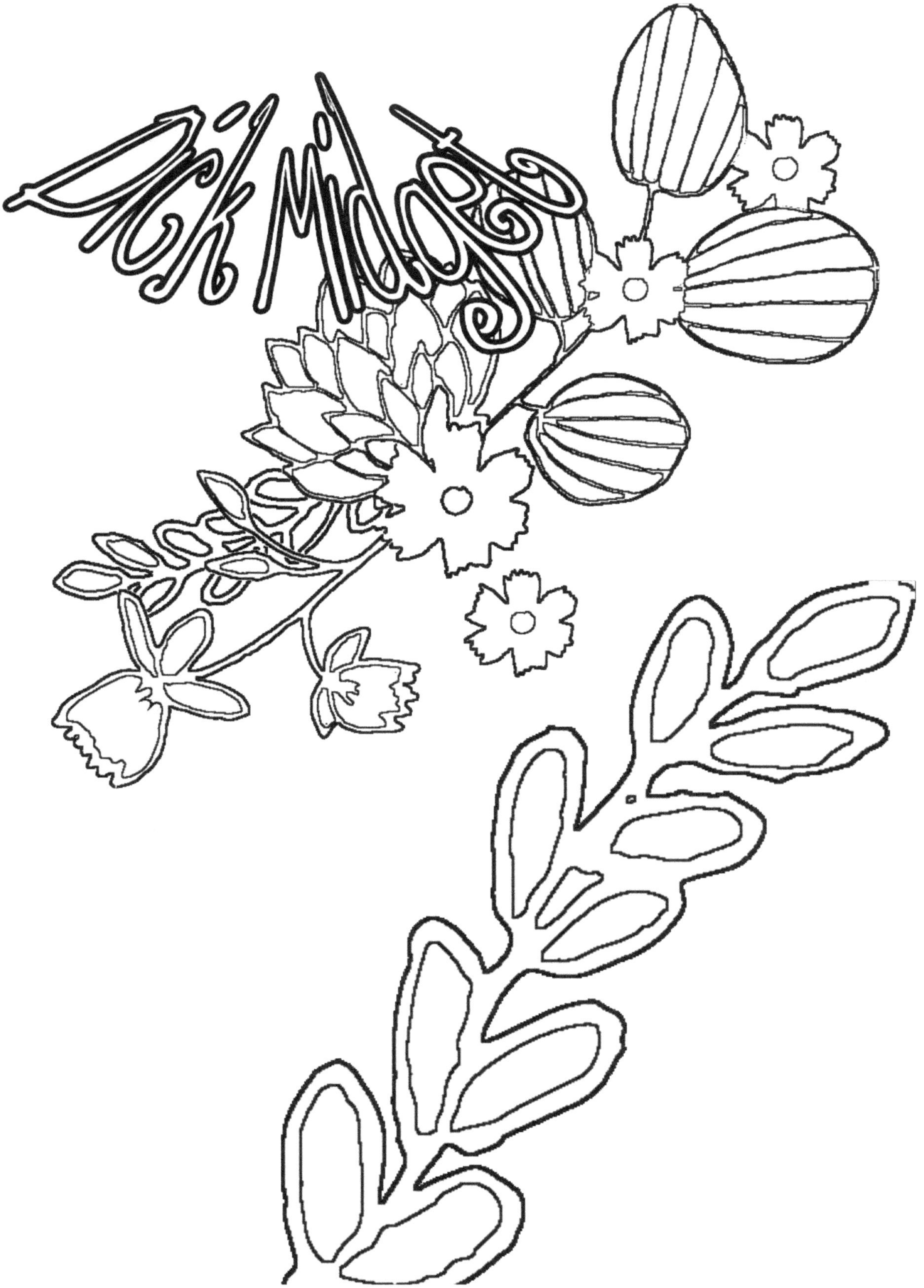
Dick Midget

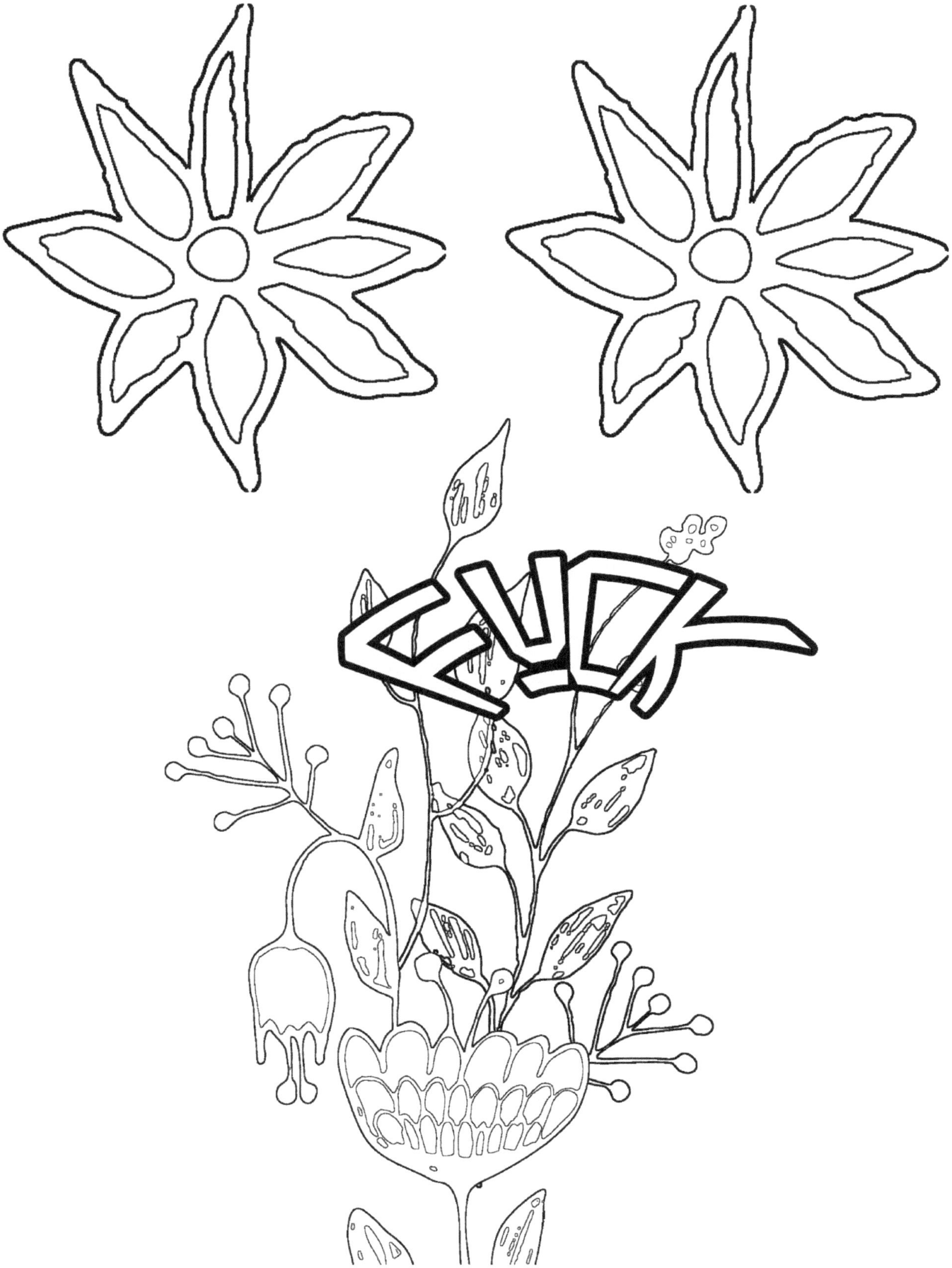
FUCK

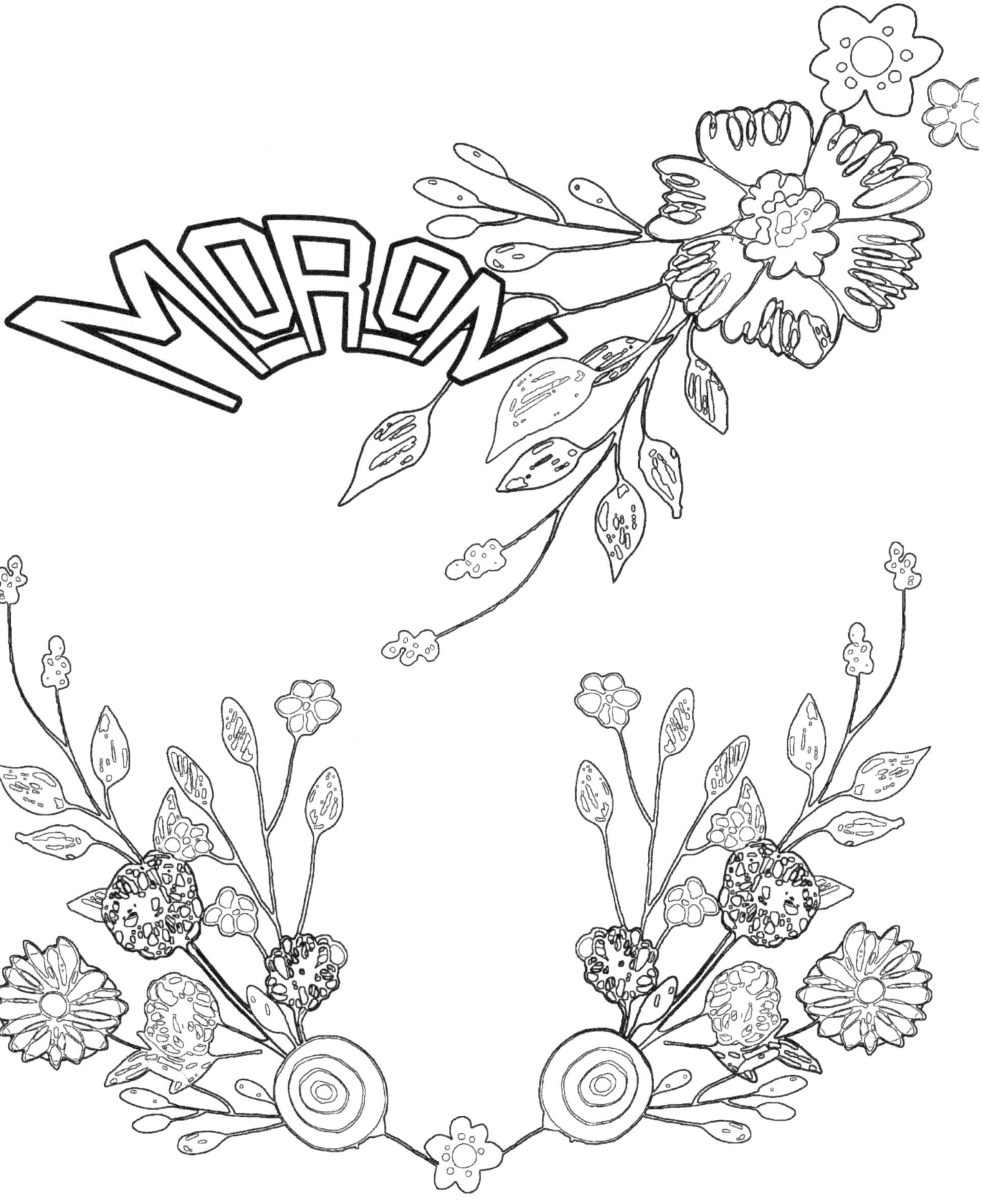
MORON

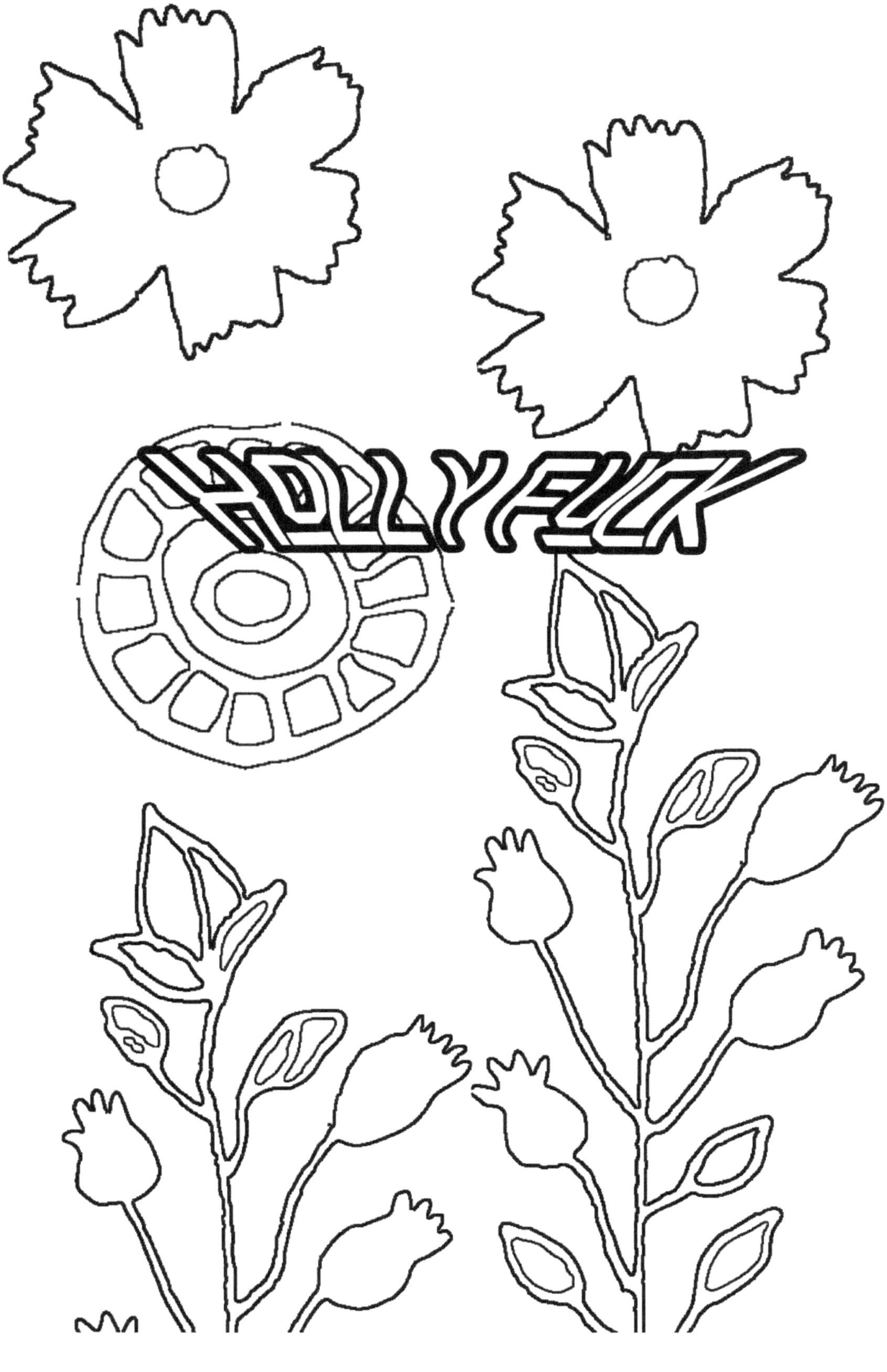
HOLLYFUCK

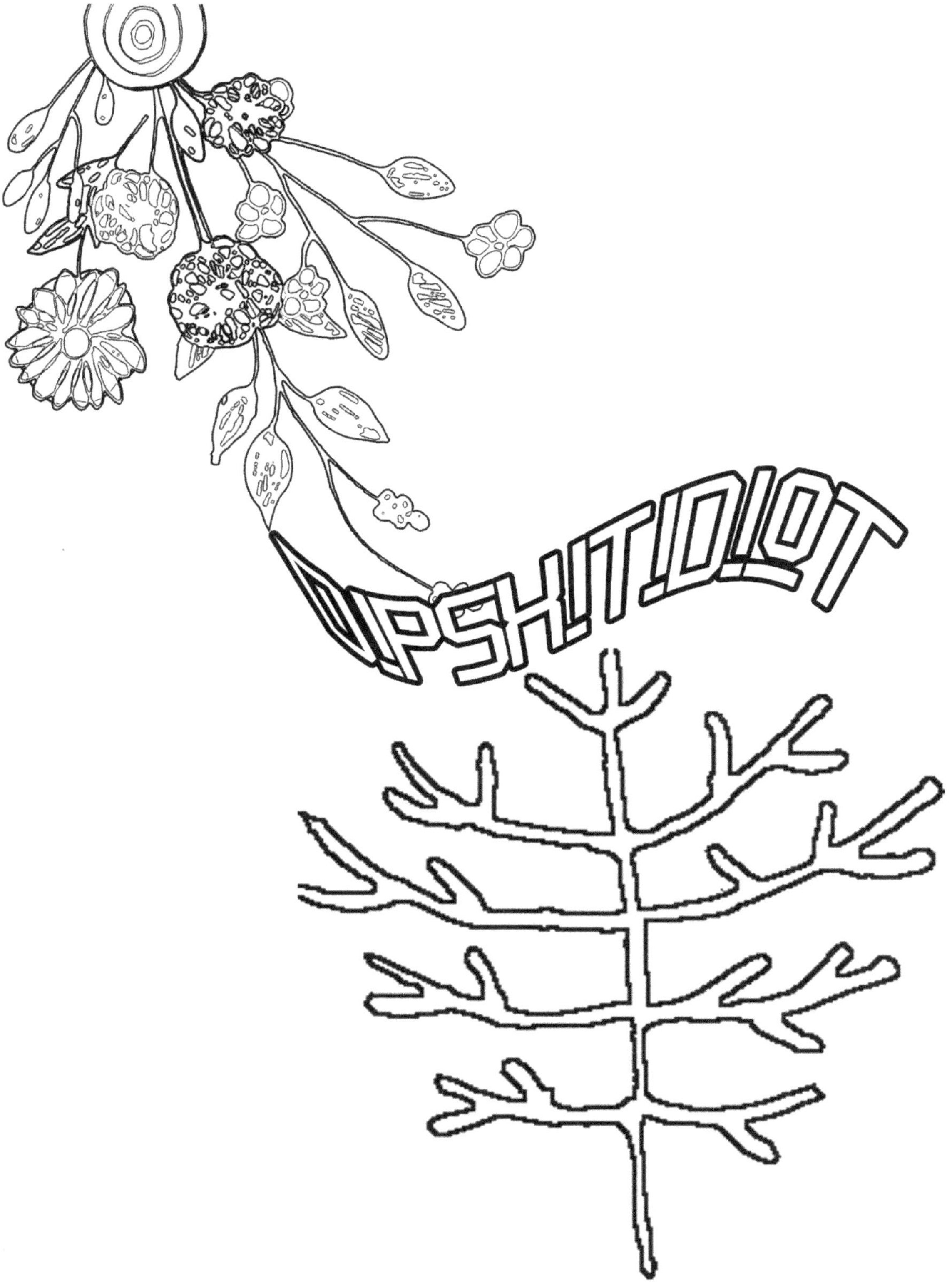
DIPSH!T ID!OT

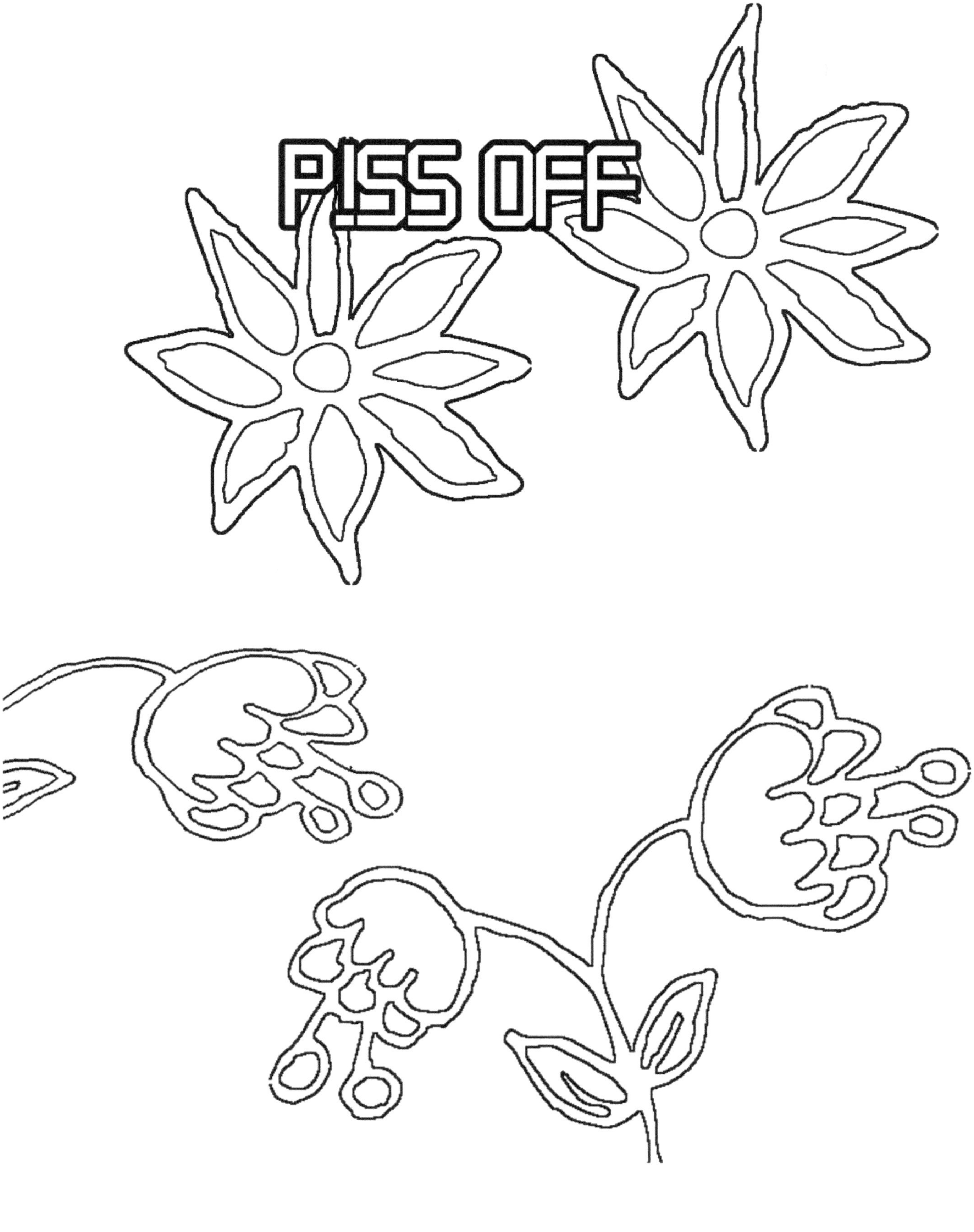
PISS OFF

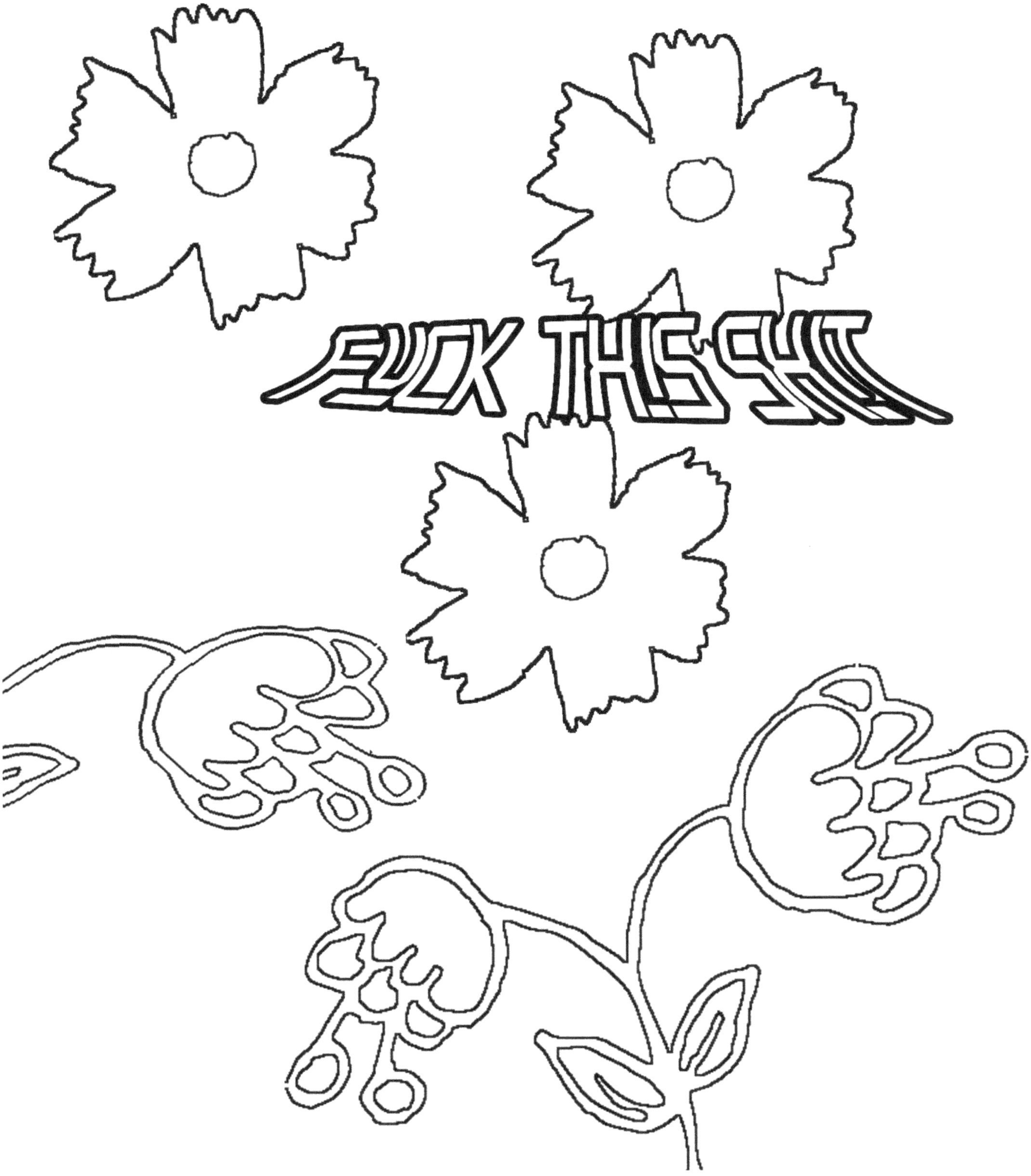
FUCK THIS SHIT

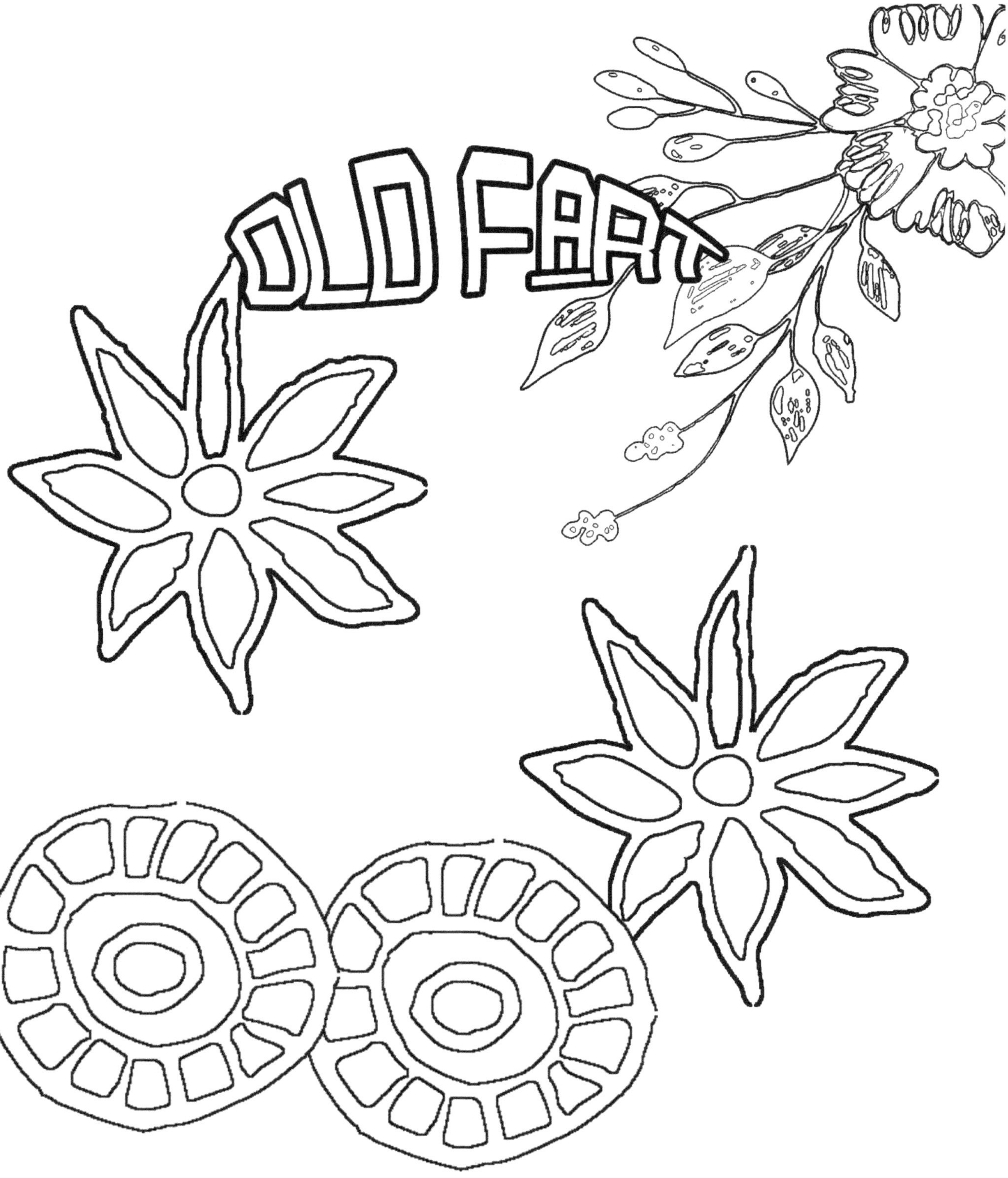
OLD FART

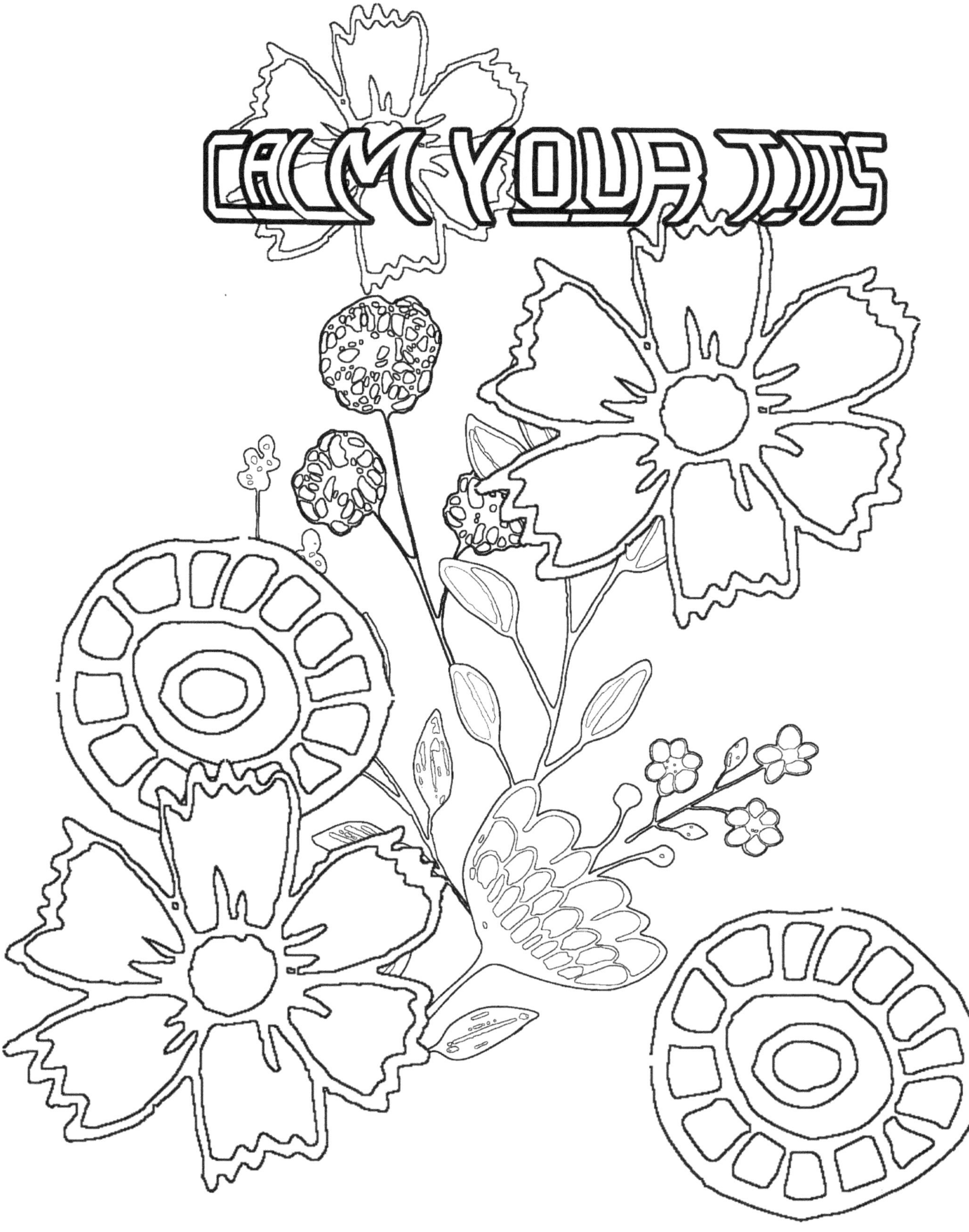
CALM YOUR TITS

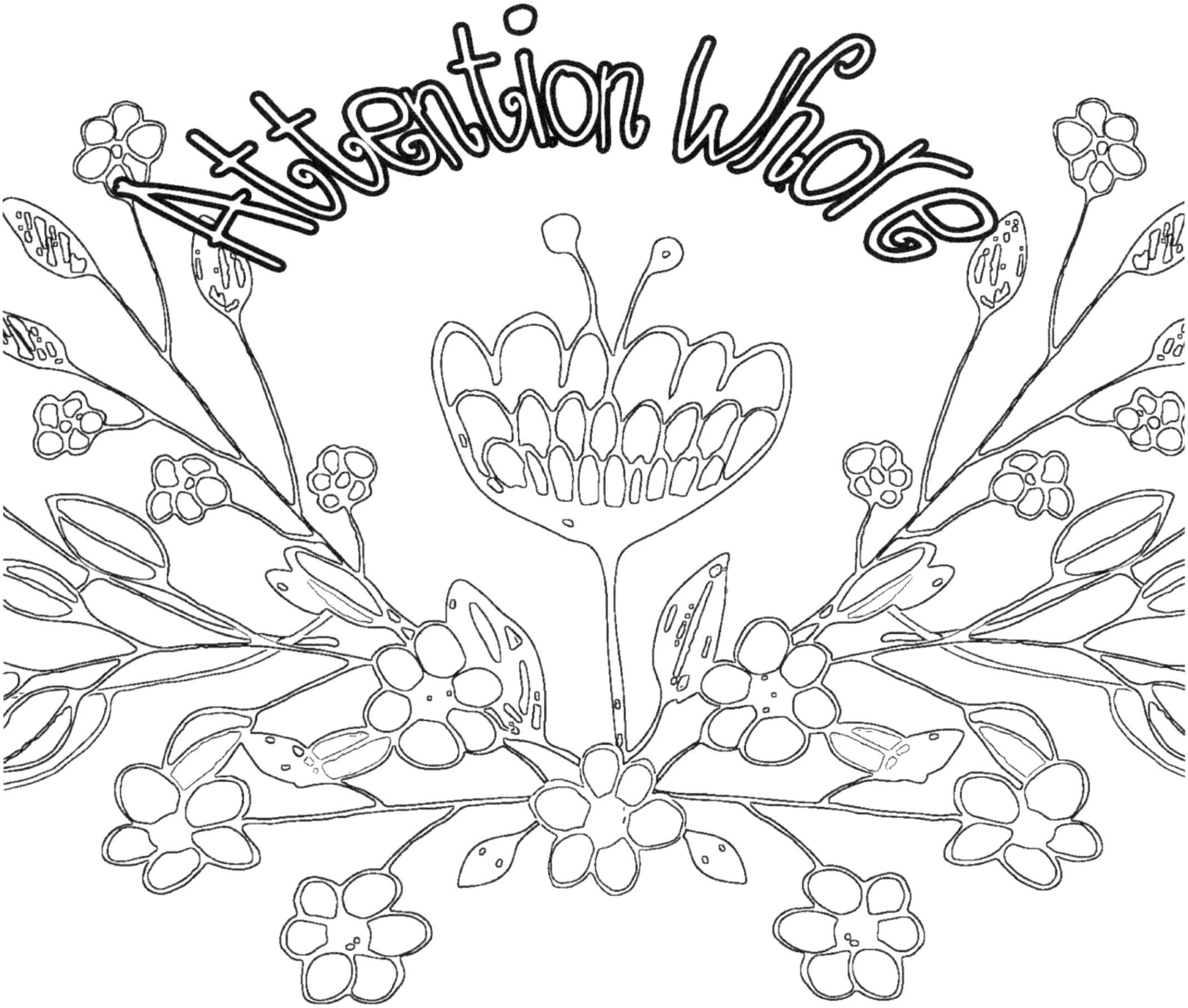
Attention Whore

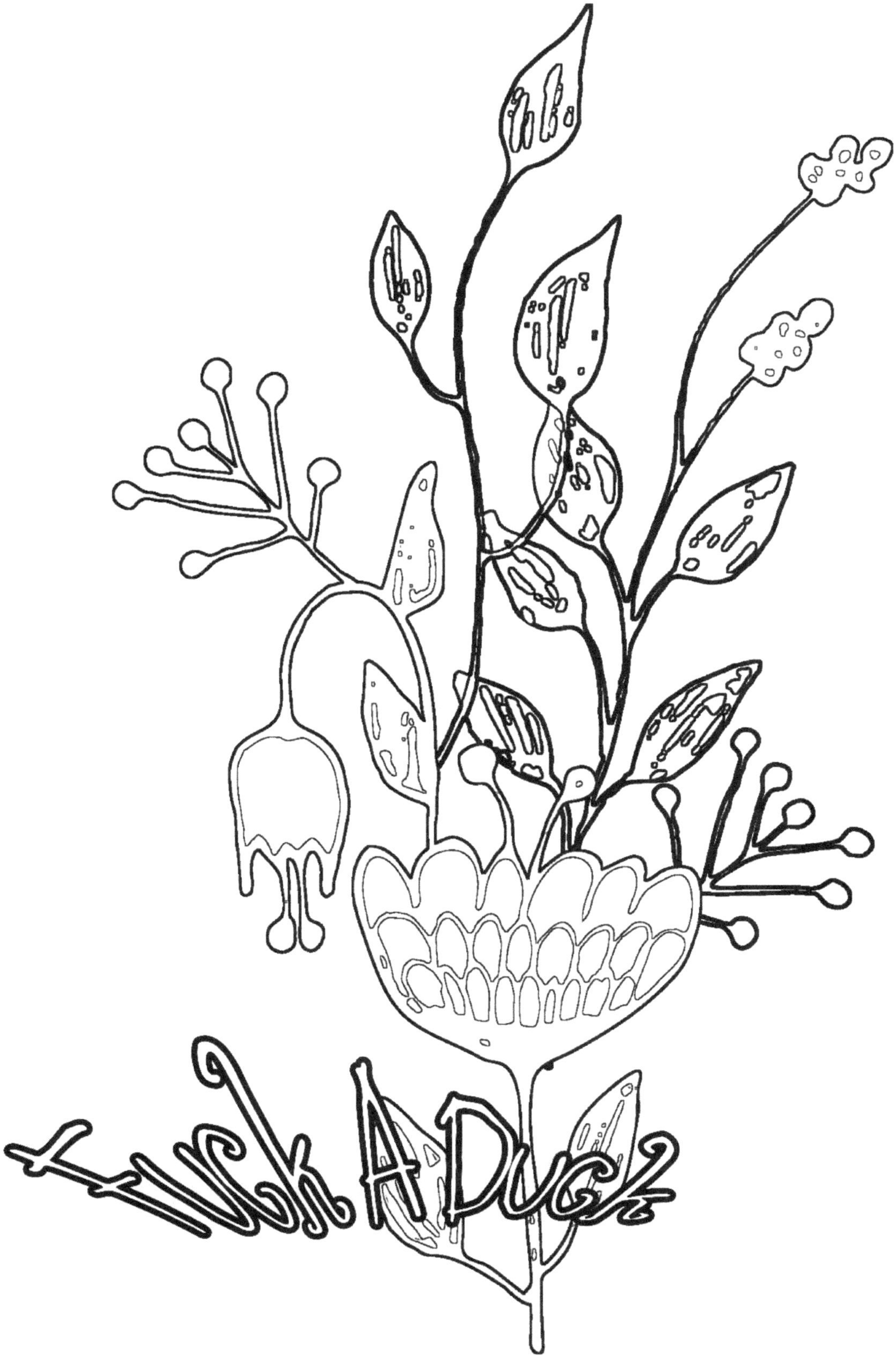
Fuck A Duck

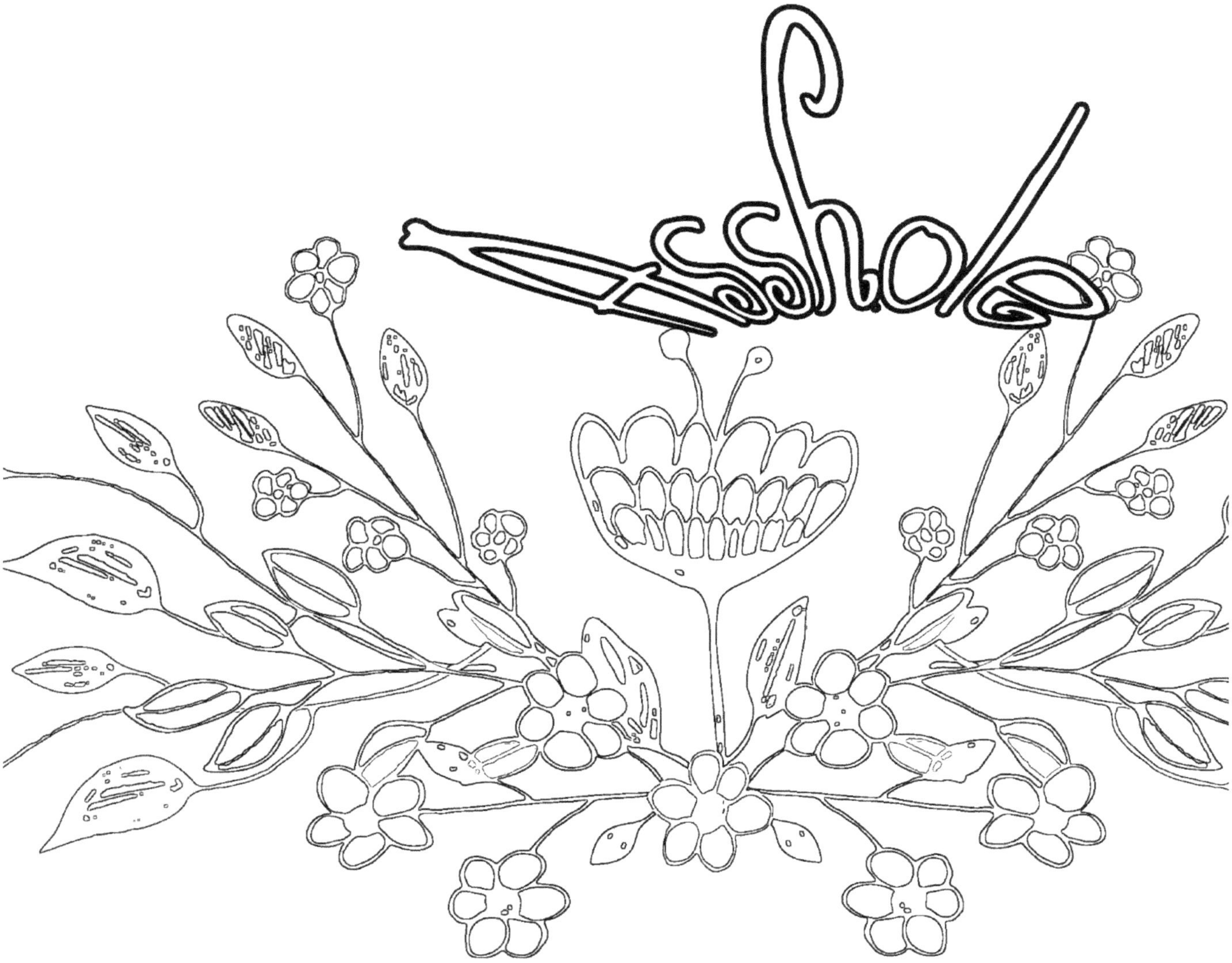
Asshole

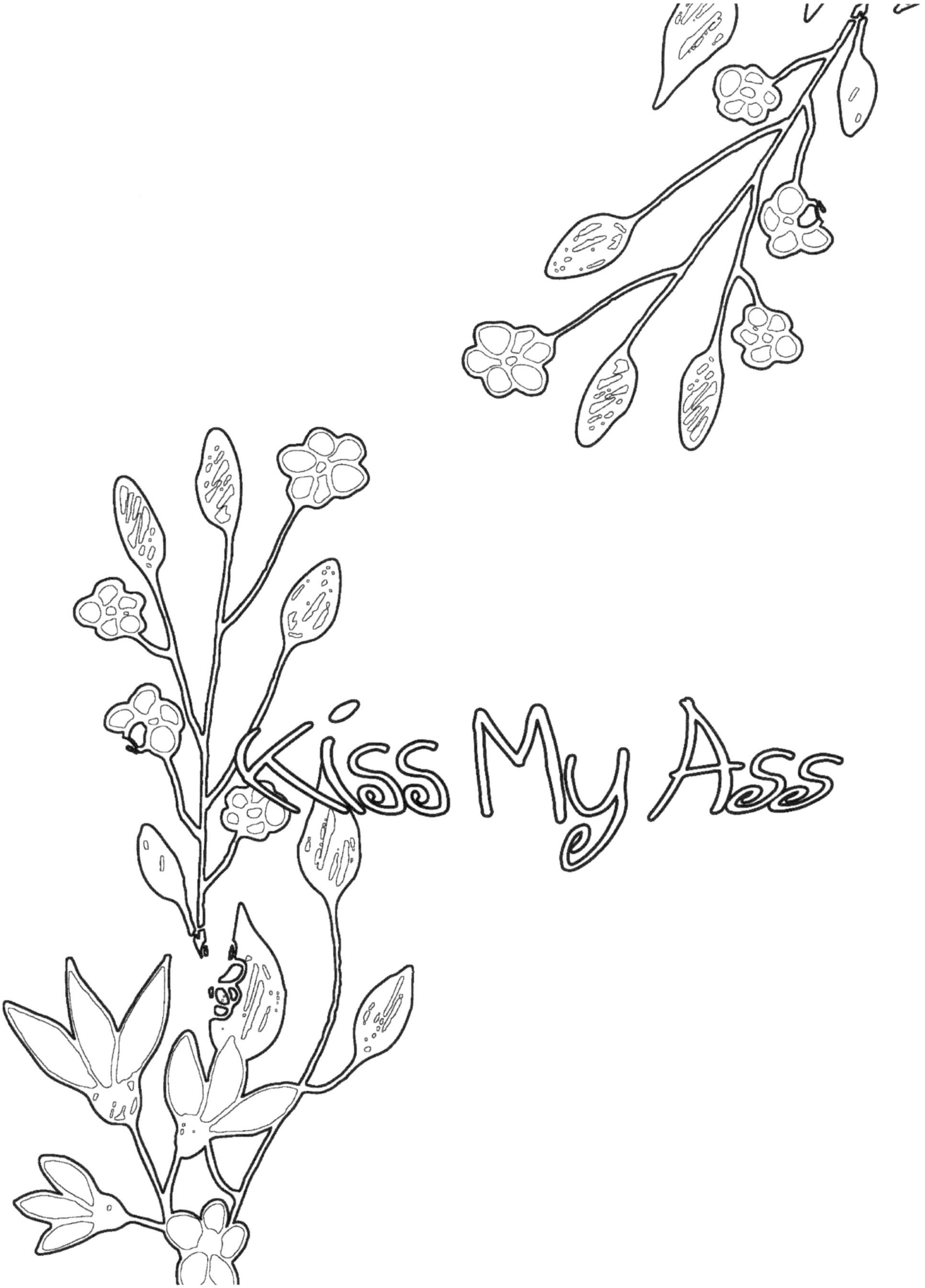
Kiss My Ass

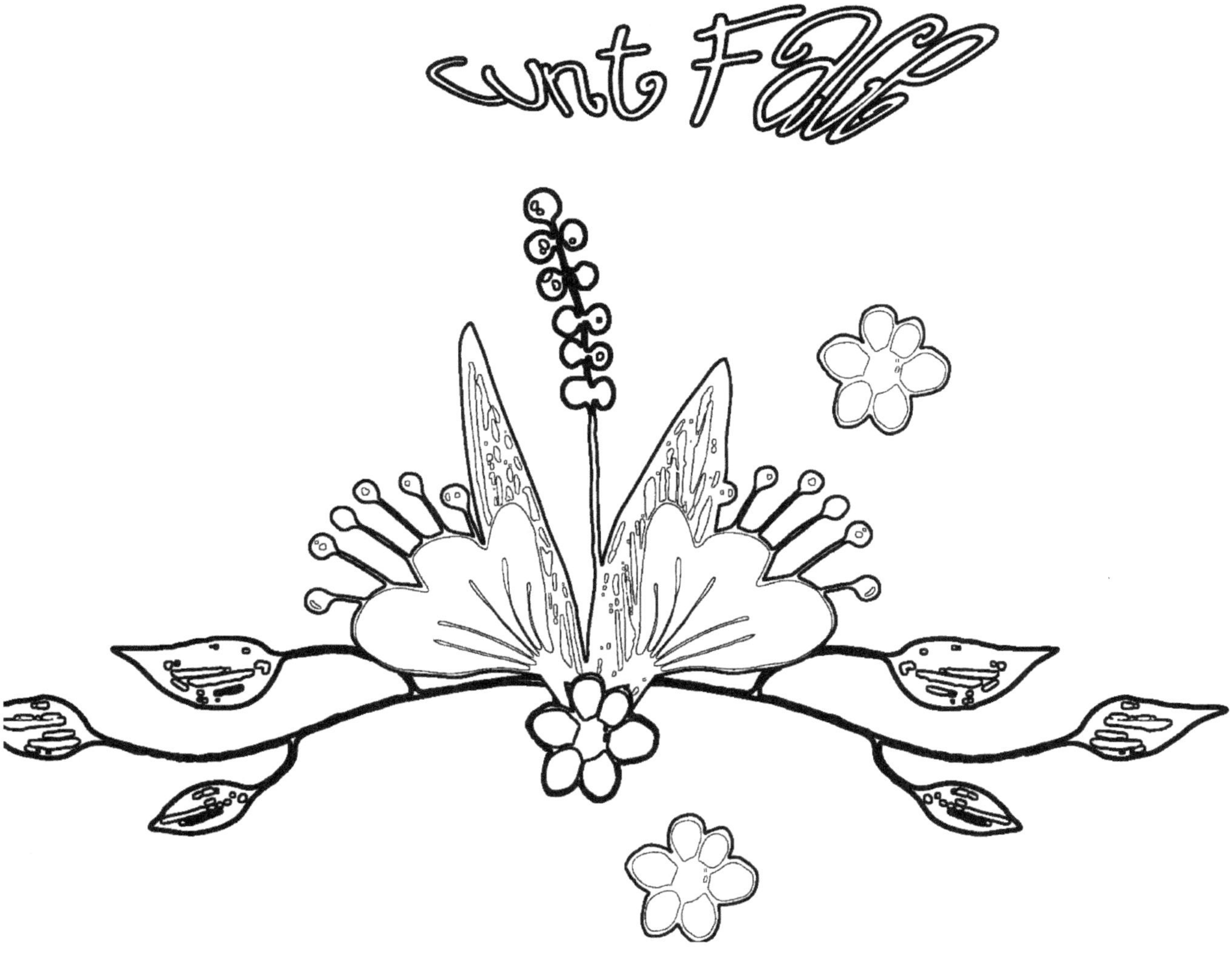
cunt

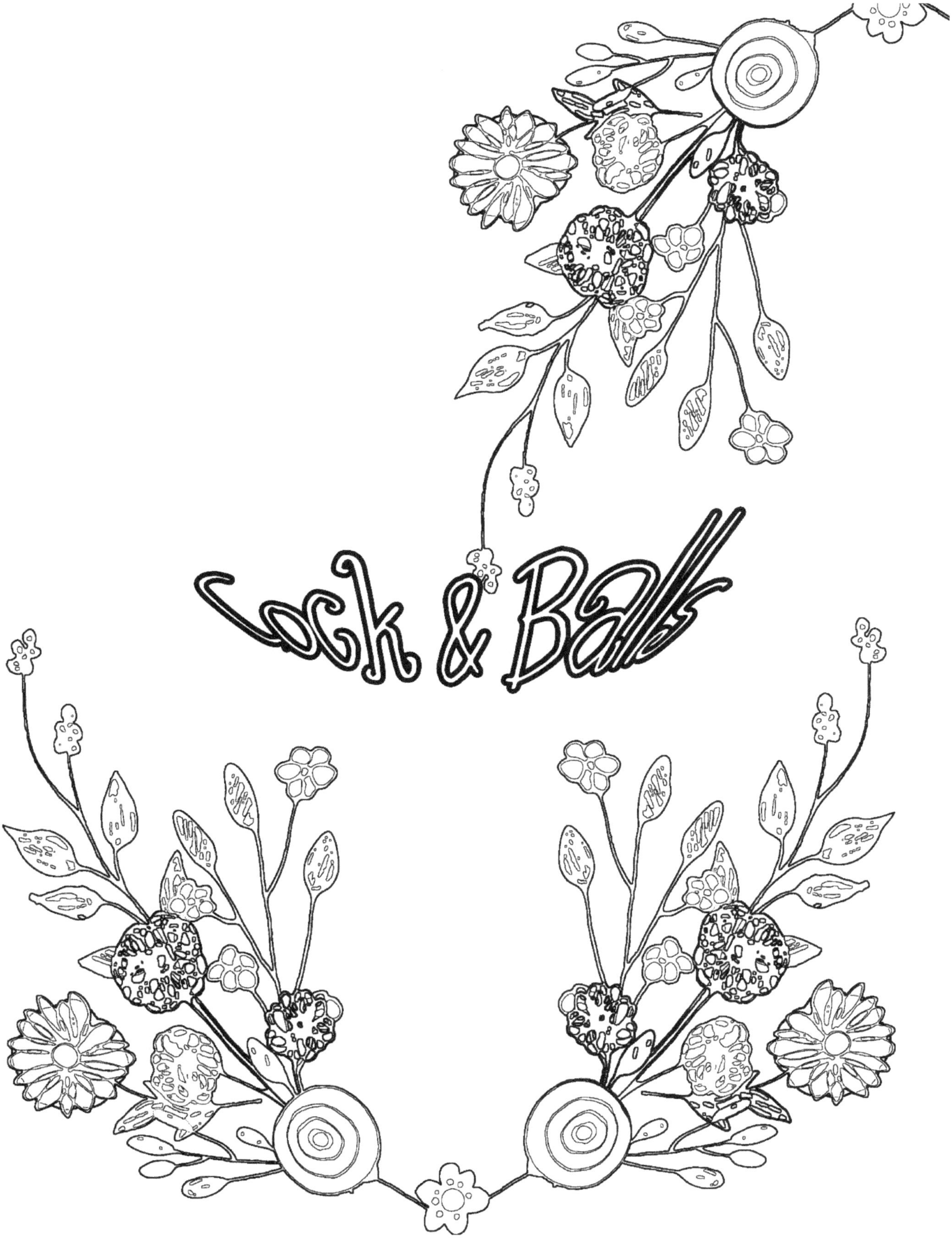
Cock & Balls

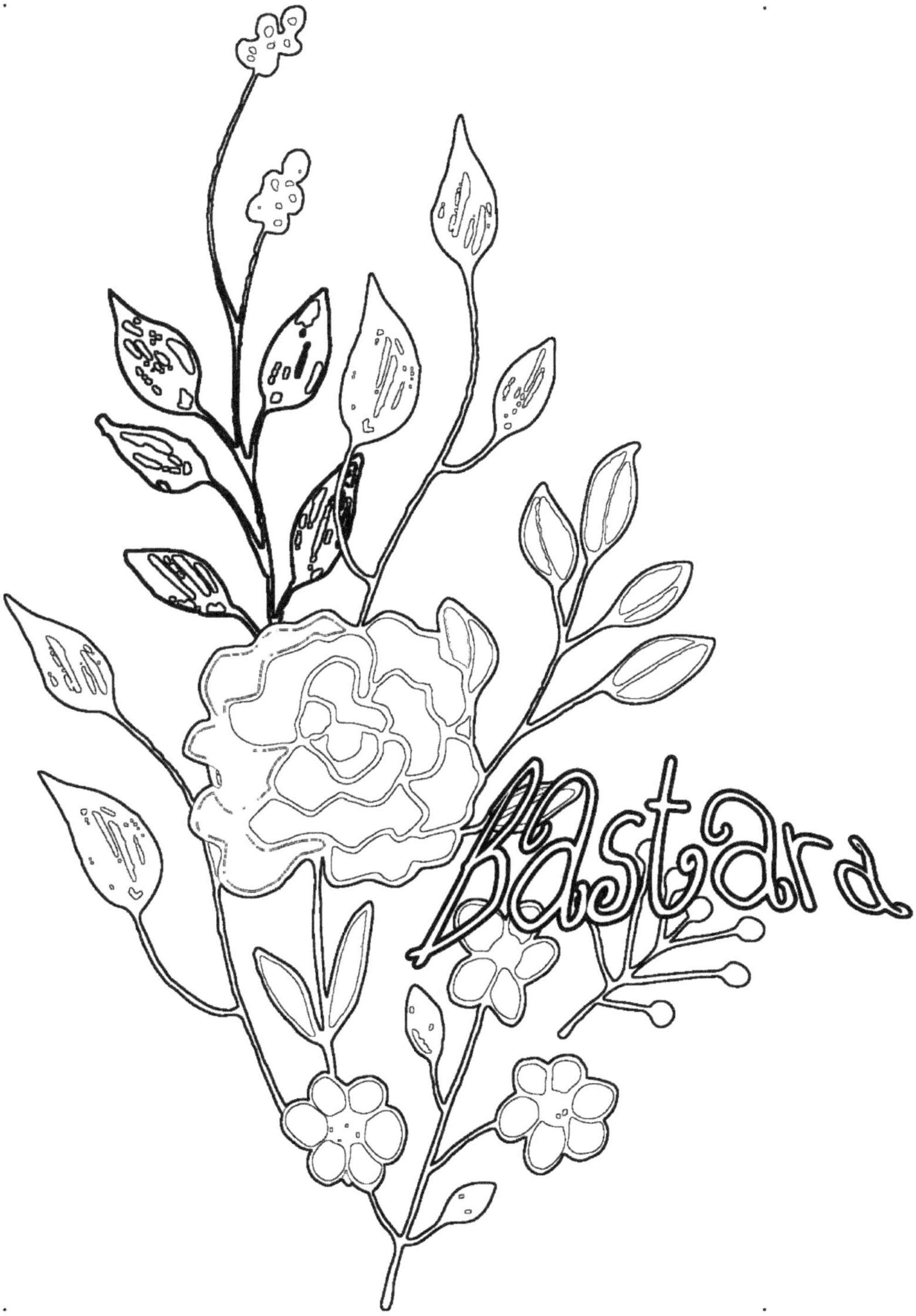
Bastard

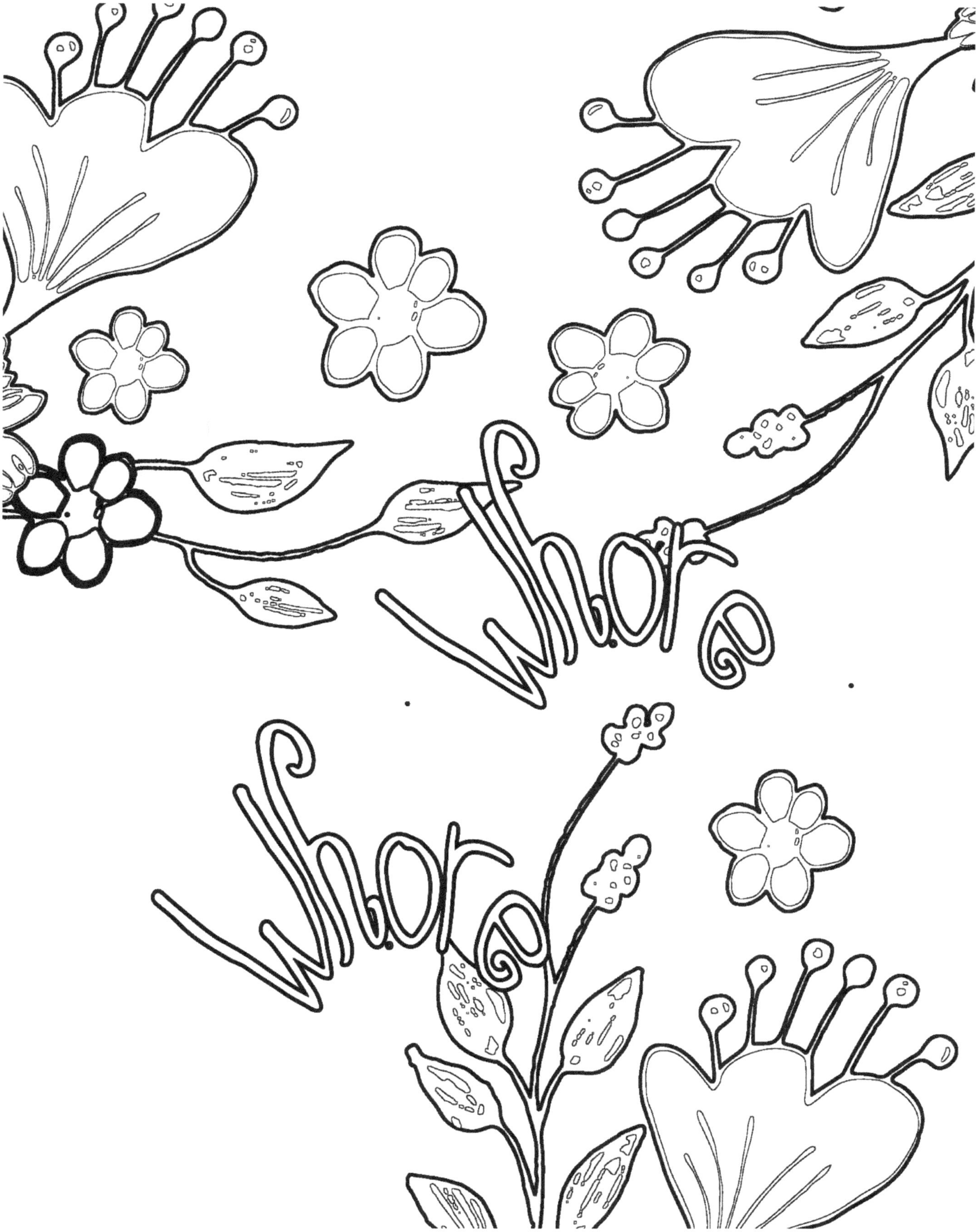
Whore
Whore

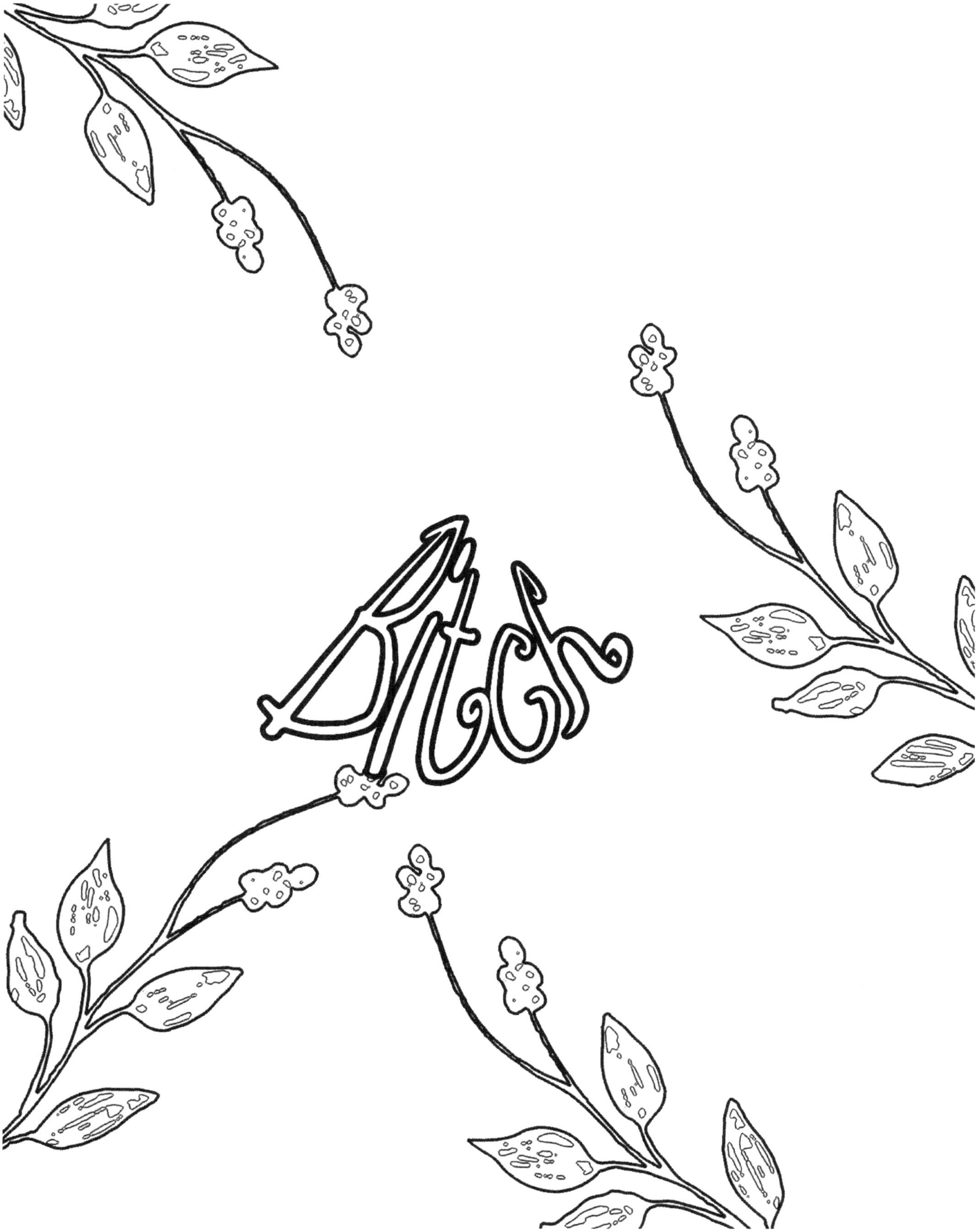
Bitch

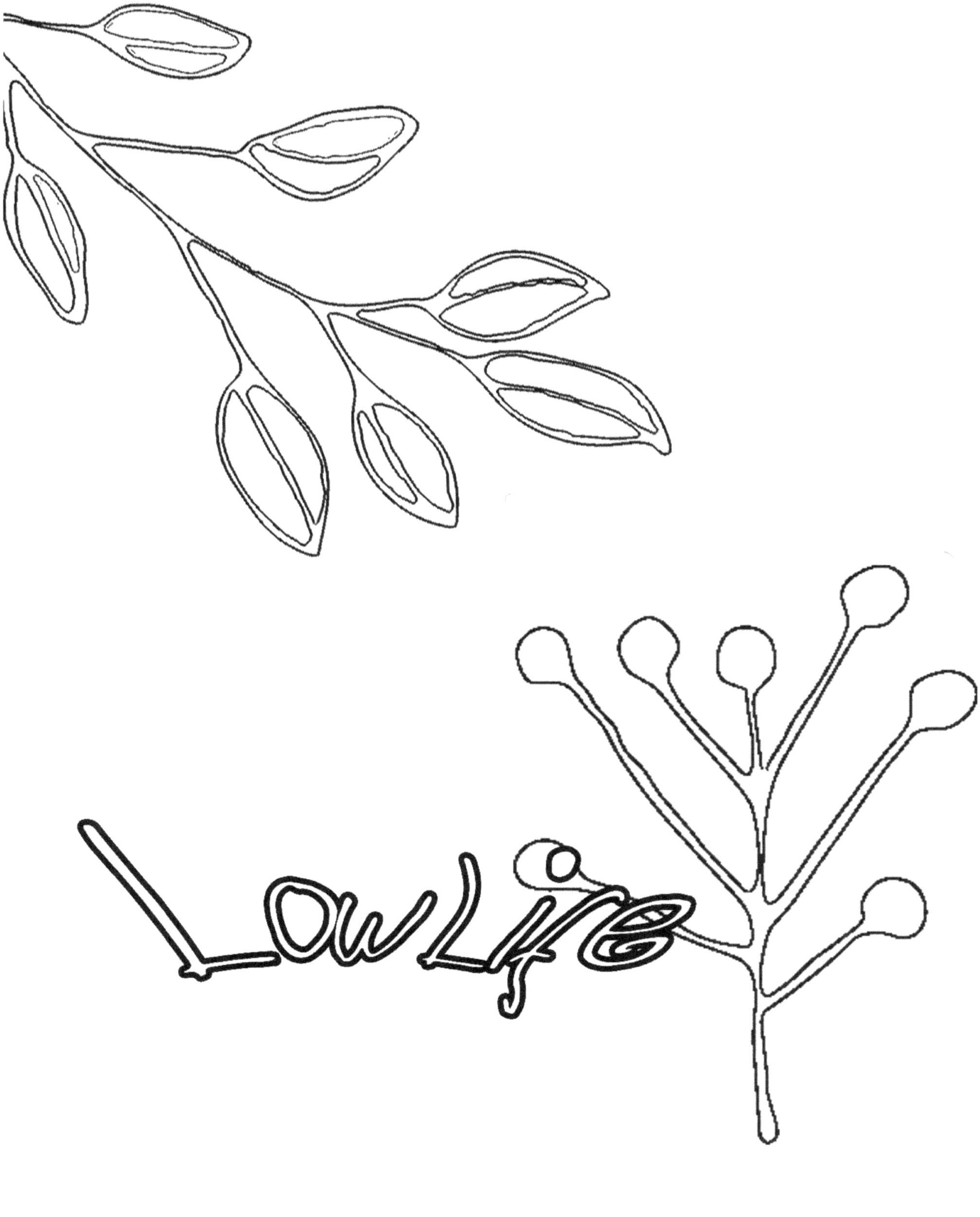
LowLife

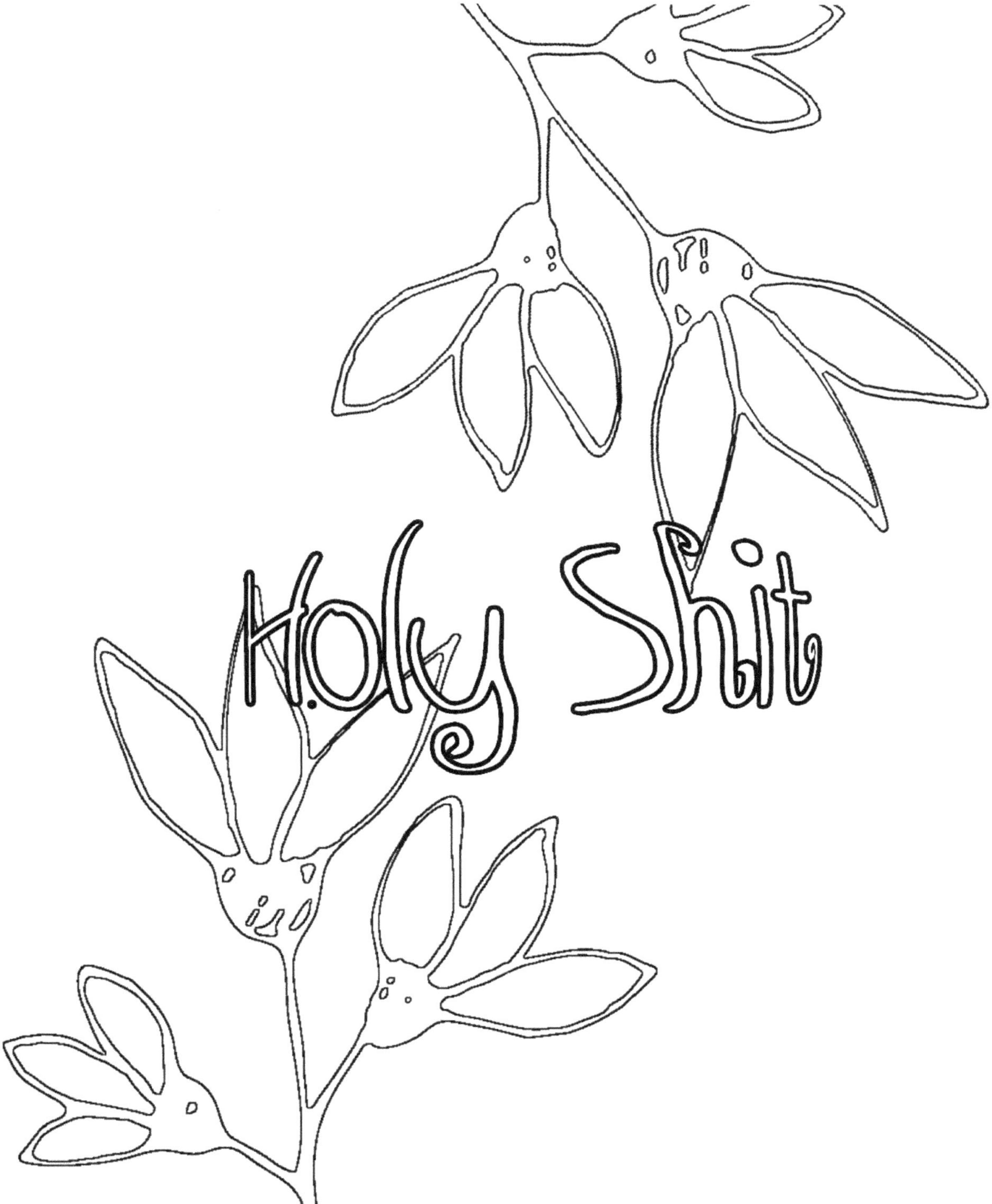
Holy Shit

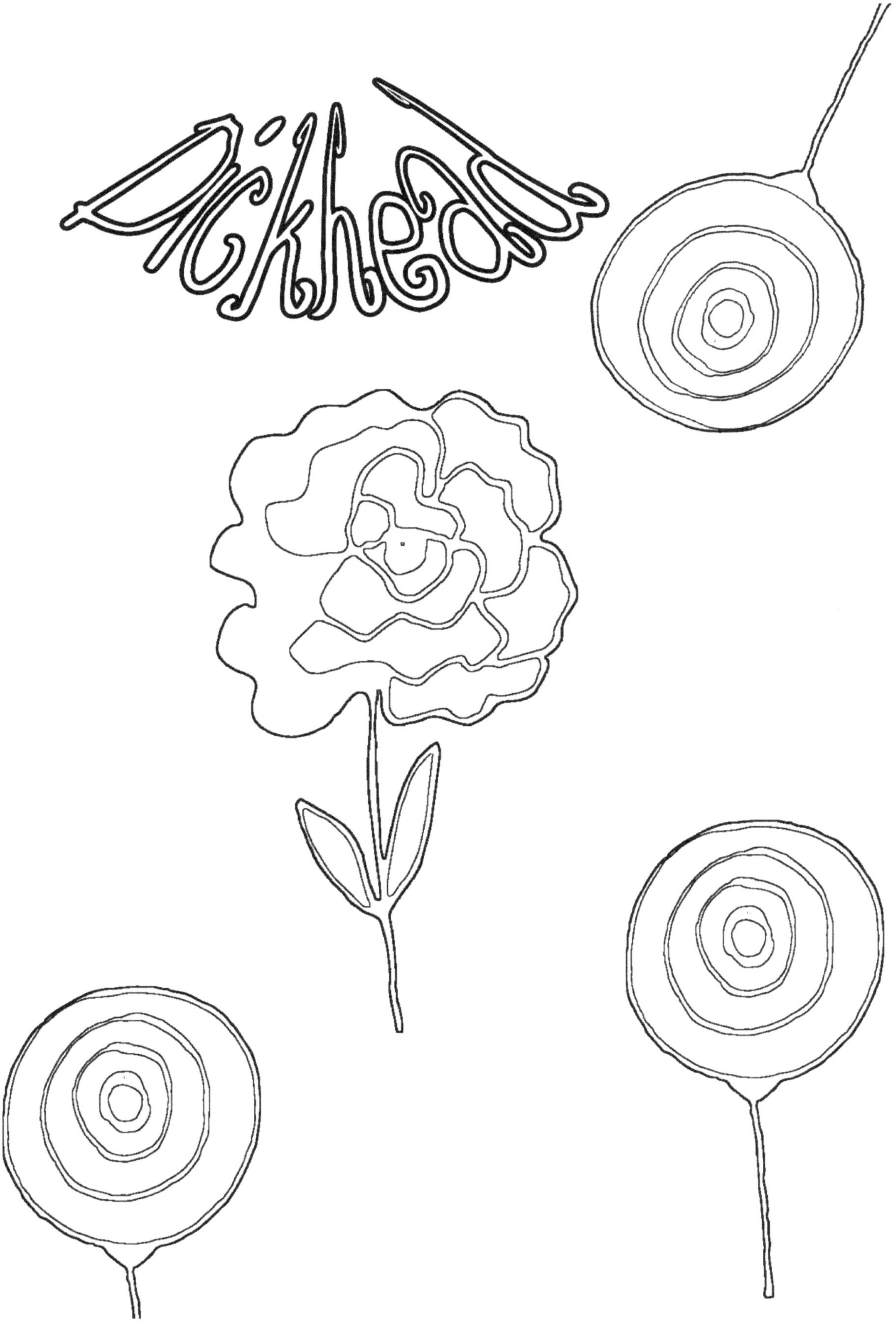
Dickhead

MOTHERFUCKER

www.ingramcontent.com/pod-product-compliance
Lightning Source LLC
Chambersburg PA
CBHW081747170526
45167CB00009B/3955
* 9 7 8 1 5 4 2 8 0 9 9 4 8 *